Abounding Love

A TREASURY OF WISDOM

EDITED, WITH COMMENTARY, BY

M. Scott Peck, M.D.

AUTHOR OF THE ROAD LESS TRAVELED

ACKNOWLEDGMENT

Since a number of quotes in this anthology were gathered from *Lessons at the Halfway Point: Wisdom for Midlife* by Michael Levine, I would specifically like to thank my friend, Michael, for donating them to this work. They are, however, copyrighted by him, and are not for general use without his permission.

02 03 04 05 06 KWF 10 9 8 7 6 5 4 3 2 1

ISBN: 0-7407-2948-9

Library of Congress Catalog Card Number: 2002103798

contents

preface

In 2000, M. Scott Peck edited a collection of his favorite quotations in a beautiful volume called *Abounding Grace: An Anthology of Wisdom*. These words, gleaned from writers and thinkers, both famous and obscure, ancient and modern, were chosen to serve as guideposts on the road to a more spiritual existence.

Abounding Love is developed from one of the twelve sections of *Abounding Grace*. The book not only includes all the quotations from the Love section of *Abounding Grace* and Dr. Peck's introductory commentary, but a number of new quotations as well.

introduction

$\mathcal{L}$OVE IS FILLED with strange twists and turns, the vast majority of which cannot be captured in the quotes to follow, much less in this brief introduction.

Gale D. Webbe, an Episcopal priest of great power, once wrote, "The further one grows spiritually, the more and more people one loves and the fewer and fewer one likes." This is inevitable. The further we grow the more we outstrip our peers, whereupon they cease to be our psychospiritual peers. And we can only like our peers, no matter how their number might be declining. Affection is mostly an emotion between equals. On the other hand, we can love virtually anyone if we set our minds to it. But there is little that is warm and bubbly about it. Liking or affection is primarily a feeling; love is primarily a matter of decision and action.

Kurt Vonnegut coined two neologisms that were very useful to me in my practice of psychotherapy: *karass* and *granfalloon*. By *granfalloon* he meant an essentially meaningless grouping. The example he gave was Hoosiers—people who just happened to reside in the state of Indiana. He defined a *karass,* to the contrary, as a truly meaningful group. An example I would give is the board of directors of the Foundation for Community Encouragement (FCE) on which my wife, Lily, and I served for a decade. We directors came from very different walks of life, but we were all leaders of one sort or another, volunteers who were called together by the same passionate commitment to spread a certain vision of community in the world.

Some of the more amusing quotes relate to the difference between friends and relatives or friends and neighbors. This is because families and neighbors are so often types of *granfalloons*. It was helpful to probably half of my patients when I explained that their families were *granfalloons*. What a relief it was for them to discover that they were not necessarily obliged to *like* their parents or their siblings! Strangely, this discovery often made it easier for them to *love* these same relatives, to provide for them with care insofar as it was in their power to do so.

The reader may be surprised to note that almost none of the quotes that follow have anything to do with romantic love. This is not an accident. Romantic love is not a virtue; it is a wonderfully pleasant feeling, possibly a purely genetic phenomenon, to facilitate mating, but often misleading and inevitably temporary. There are so many illusions about love that I felt I had no choice in *The Road Less Traveled* but to begin its lengthy section on the subject by proclaiming all the things that genuine love is not. One of them was romantic love. Although I have received over ten thousand letters in response to that book, only one took issue with my proclamation that the bloom of romance always fades; its author was twenty-two years of age.

Then what is genuine love? In that same book I was bold enough to define it as "the will to extend one's self for the purpose of nurturing one's own or another's spiritual growth." But, by God's grace, I had the humility to conclude my discussion of the subject with a subsection entitled "The Mystery of Love," citing some of the ways and reasons that my definition was utterly inadequate.

My wife and I have been wed for forty years now. That is a long time for a sustained, intimate relationship. Much of that time was not particularly pleasant. During it we have gone through all the classical stages of death and dying, as elucidated by Elisabeth Kübler-Ross: denial, anger, bargaining, depression, and acceptance. First we went to great pains to deny that the bloom of our romantic love had faded. When that didn't work and we were faced with our profound differences (which, of course, we perceived as faults) we became angry at each other—and even angrier as we attempted without success to somehow change or "heal" the other. When this strategy failed, we went through a phase of bargaining in which we attempted to develop formulas for working around each other's faults—a phase of negotiation that was without joy. Joyless, we then descended into a lengthy phase of depression wherein each of us seriously wondered, with little hope, whether it was worth it at all. Yet finally and

One answer is that we've had a large number of shared passions ranging from delight in spicy food to delight in travel to foreign lands in order to search for strange and ancient stone monuments. But I believe our most powerful shared passion has been for our own psychospiritual growth. We even attempt to transmit this to others. Indeed, the most common complaint of our staff is: "Oh, no, not the 'G' word again!" Such growth is clearly not everyone's bag. Yet over these years both Lily and I have grown— changed—and, as a result, we've remained interesting to each other. I'm not sure our marriage could have survived without this consistent element of surprise, the element that has continued to keep us "peers," thereby maintaining our mutual affection.

Still, there is something even deeper. As I've so often stated, all the virtues are intertwined, and I believe more powerful than our shared passions have been our shared gifts: compassion, commitment, loyalty, perseverance, and so on. Add all these virtues up, and they can be summed into one: love. Not romantic love but prosaic love. Our marriage has not only survived its vicissitudes but generally overcome them through our prosaic, daily love. But why have we—Lily and I—been given the gift of such love? I do not know. Once again, like all gifts, it is a mystery.

Inexplicable though it may be, there is power in it. Great power. I have suggested in other writings that this might well be a naturally evil world that has somehow been contaminated by a mysterious infection of goodness, and that the "good bugs" are multiplying. There is a name for this infection: love. The corniest quote I know is that "Love makes the world go around." It is also the only profound truth I know that is not a paradox. Were there some sort of gigantic love vacuum cleaner that could suck all the love out of the earth—all the love that God pours into it and all the love that we humans have for each other—then I fully believe this world would come to a grinding halt in a matter of hours. Yet the reality is that we keep going on, and ever so slowly we seem to be getting a bit better at it. Love is why Dame Julian of Norwich, more than six centuries ago, was enabled to pen the most outrageous proclamation of optimism ever written: "Despite . . . the inevitability of sin, all shall be well, all shall be well, and all manner of thing shall be well."

affection

Affection is created by habit, community of
interests, convenience, and the desire of
companionship. It is a comfort rather than
an exhilaration.
——W. SOMERSET MAUGHAM

'Tis sweet to feel by what fine-spun threads our
affections are drawn together.
——LAURENCE STERNE

*P*raise is well, compliment is well, but
   affection—that is the last and final and
   most precious reward that any man can win,
   whether by character or achievement.
                    —MARK TWAIN

*D*o not save your loving speeches
For your friends till they are dead;
Do not write them on their tombstones,
Speak them rather now instead.
                    —ANNA CUMMINS

*H*uman nature is so constructed that it gives
    affection most readily to those who seem least
    to demand it.
                            —BERTRAND RUSSELL

*O*ne must not be mean with affections; what
    is spent of the funds is renewed in
    the spending itself. Left untouched for too
    long, they diminish imperceptibly or the
    lock gets rusty. They are there all right,
    but one cannot make use of them.
                            —SIGMUND FREUD

*W*hat do we live for if not to make life less difficult for each other?
—GEORGE ELIOT

*W*e should measure affection, not like youngsters by the ardor of its passion, but by its strength and constancy.
—CICERO

*A*nd all people live, not by reason of any care they have for themselves, but by the love for them that is in other people.
—LEO TOLSTOY

*F*ellowship is heaven, and lack of fellowship is hell; fellowship is life, and lack of fellowship is death; and the deeds that ye do upon the earth, it is for fellowship's sake that you do them.

—WILLIAM MORRIS

*T*he happiest moments my heart knows are those in which it is pouring forth its affections to a few esteemed characters.

—THOMAS JEFFERSON

*G*ood company in a journey makes the way seem
the shorter.
—Izaak Walton

*T*he feet carry the body as affection carries
the soul.
—St. Catherine of Siena

*F*amiliarity breeds content.
—Anna Quindlen

*A*mid all the easily loved darlings of Charlie
  Brown's circle, obstreperous Lucy holds a
special place in my heart. She fusses and
fumes and she carps and complains. That's
because Lucy cares. And it's the caring that
counts. When we, as youngsters, would accuse
our mother of picking on us her wise reply
was, "All you'll get from strangers is surface
pleasantry or indifference. Only someone who
loves you will criticize you."

—JUDITH CRIST

friendship

*F*riendship is a single soul dwelling in two bodies.
—ARISTOTLE

A companion loves some agreeable qualities
which a man may possess, but a friend loves
the man himself.
—JAMES BOSWELL

Do not use a hatchet to remove a fly from your
friend's forehead.

—CHINESE PROVERB

Friendships, like marriages, are dependent on
avoiding the unforgivable.

—JOHN D. MACDONALD

A man must eat a peck of salt with his friend
before he knows him.

—CERVANTES

*I*t is one of the blessings of old friends that you
can afford to be stupid with them.

—RALPH WALDO EMERSON

*W*e do not so much need the help of our friends
as the confidence of their help in need.

—EPICURUS

*O*ne's friends are that part of the human race
with which one can be human.

—GEORGE SANTAYANA

*I*n politics . . . shared hatreds are almost always
the basis of friendships.

—ALEXIS DE TOCQUEVILLE

*Y*our friend is the man who knows all about you,
and still likes you.

—ELBERT HUBBARD

*T*here can be no friendship where there is no free-
dom. Friendship loves a free air, and will not
be fenced up in straight and narrow enclosures.

—WILLIAM PENN

*W*hen my friends are one-eyed, I look at them
   in profile.
                              —ELBERT HUBBARD

*G*reat souls by instinct to each other turn,
Demand alliance, and in friendship burn.
                              —JOSEPH ADDISON

*I*f a man should importune me to give a reason
   why I loved him, I find it could not otherwise
   be expressed, than by making answer: because
   it was he, because it was I.
                              —MICHEL DE MONTAIGNE

*F*riendship either finds or makes equals.

—PUBLILIUS SYRUS

*L*ife is nothing without friendship.

—QUINTUS ENNIUS

*F*riendship's the wine of life.

—EDWARD YOUNG

*G*reater love hath no man than this, that a man lay down his life for his friends.

—JOHN 15:13

*S*ooner or later you've heard all your best friends have to say. Then comes the tolerance of real love.

—NED ROREM

*F*riendship cannot live with ceremony, nor without civility.

—LORD HALIFAX

*F*riendship is the marriage of the soul; and this marriage is subject to divorce.

—VOLTAIRE

*T*rue friendship is a plant of slow growth and must
undergo and withstand the shocks of adversity
before it is entitled to the appellation.
—GEORGE WASHINGTON

*Y*ou can win more friends with your ears than
your mouth.
—ANONYMOUS

*B*etween friends there is no need of justice.
—ARISTOTLE

The bird a nest, the spider a web, man friendship.
—WILLIAM BLAKE

Those who have suffered understand suffering and
therefore extend their hand.
—PATTI SMITH

Being considerate of others will take you and
your children further in life than any college
or professional degree.
—MARIAN WRIGHT EDELMAN

I find friendship to be like wine, raw when new, ripened with age, the true old man's milk and restorative cordial.

—THOMAS JEFFERSON

*F*riendship closes its eyes rather than see the moon eclipse; while malice denies that it is ever at the full.

—JULIUS CHARLES HARE AND
AUGUSTUS WILLIAM HARE

*T*he only way to have a friend is to be one.

—RALPH WALDO EMERSON

The easiest kind of relationship for me is with ten
thousand people. The hardest is with one.
—JOAN BAEZ

If I had to choose between betraying my *country*
and betraying my *friend*, I hope I should have
the guts to betray my country.
—E. M. FORSTER

Friends are God's apology for relations.
—HUGH KINGSMILL

Friends are born, not made.
—HENRY ADAMS

People's lives change. To keep all your old
friends is like keeping all your old clothes—
pretty soon your closet is so jammed and everything so crushed you can't find anything to
wear. Help these friends when they need you;
bless the years and happy times when you
meant a lot to each other, but try *not* to have
the guilts if new people mean more to you now.
—HELEN GURLEY BROWN

I have lost friends, some by death . . . others
through sheer inability to cross the street.
—VIRGINIA WOOLF

The person who tries to live alone will not succeed
as a human being. His heart withers if it does
not answer another heart. His mind shrinks
away if he hears only the echos of his own
thoughts and finds no other inspiration.
—PEARL S. BUCK

Real friendship is shown in times of trouble;
prosperity is full of friends.
—EURIPIDES

*W*ithout reciprocal mildness and temperance there can be no continuance of friendship. Every man will have something to do for his friend, and something to bear with in him.

— OWEN FELLTHAM

*G*od gives us our relatives; thank God we can choose our friends!

— ETHEL WATTS MUMFORD

A good friend is my nearest relation.

— THOMAS FULLER, M.D.

*N*o person is your friend who demands your
silence, or denies your right to grow.
——ALICE WALKER

*E*ach friend represents a world in us, a world
possibly not born until they arrive, and it is
only by this meeting that a new world is born.
——ANAÏS NIN

A friend can tell you things you don't want to
tell yourself.
——FRANCES WARD WELLER

I can trust my friends. . . . These people force me to examine myself, encourage me to grow.

—CHER

*I*t takes two to make a quarrel, but only one to end it.

—SPANISH PROVERB

*N*ine-tenths of the people were created so you would want to be with the other tenth.

—HORACE WALPOLE

*I*n a world more and more polluted by the lying of politicians and the illusions of the media, I occasionally crave to hear and tell the truth. To borrow a beautiful phrase from Friedrich Nietzsche, I look upon my friend as "the beautiful enemy" who alone is able to offer me total candor. Friendship is by its very nature freer of deceit than any other relationship we can know because it is the bond least affected by striving for power, physical pleasure, or material profit, most liberated from any oath of duty or of constancy.

—FRANCINE DU PLESSIX GRAY

Shared joy is double joy, and shared sorrow is half-sorrow.

———Swedish proverb

Yes'm, old friends is always best, 'less you can catch a new one that's fit to make an old one out of.

———Sarah Orne Jewett

Friendship with oneself is all-important, because without it one cannot be friends with anyone else in the world.

———Eleanor Roosevelt

*T*wo may talk together under the same roof for many years, yet never really meet; and two others at first speech are old friends.

—MARY CATHERWOOD

A friend i' the court is better than a penny in the purse.

—WILLIAM SHAKESPEARE

*W*ishing to be friends is quick work, but friendship is a slow-ripening fruit.

—ARISTOTLE

Old friends are best. King James used to call for his old shoes; they were easiest for his feet.
——JOHN SELDEN

Before borrowing money from a friend decide which you need most.
——AMERICAN PROVERB

Friendship admits of difference of character, as love does that of sex.
——JOSEPH ROUX

A man cannot be said to succeed in this life who does not satisfy one friend.
——HENRY DAVID THOREAU

A true friend is one who likes you despite your achievements.
——ARNOLD BENNETT

I like a friend the better for having faults that one can talk about.
——WILLIAM HAZLITT

The ornament of a house is the friends who
frequent it.
—RALPH WALDO EMERSON

The man that hails you Tom or Jack,
And proves by thumps upon your back
How he esteems your merit,
Is such a friend, that one had need
Be very much his friend indeed
To pardon or to bear it.
—WILLIAM COWPER

I pretend ivry man is honest, and I believe none iv them ar-re. In that way I keep me friends an' save me money.

—FINLEY PETER DUNNE

I have no trouble with my enemies. But my goddam friends, . . . they are the ones that keep me walking the floor nights.

—WARREN G. HARDING

I nstead of loving your enemies, treat your friends a little better.

—EDGAR HOWE

In prosperity our friends know us; in adversity we
know our friends.
—CHURTON COLLINS

Every man passes his life in the search after
friendship.
—RALPH WALDO EMERSON

A friend should bear his friend's infirmities.
—WILLIAM SHAKESPEARE

The shifts of fortune test the reliability of friends.
—CICERO

Think where man's glory most begins and ends
And say my glory was I had such friends.
—WILLIAM BUTLER YEATS

You can hardly make a friend in a year, but you
can easily offend one in an hour.
—CHINESE PROVERB

You can make more friends in two months by
becoming more interested in other people than
you can in two years by trying to get people
interested in you.
—DALE CARNEGIE

*I*t is well, when one is judging a friend, to
remember that he is judging you with the
same godlike and superior impartiality.
—ARNOLD BENNETT

*T*here are three faithful friends—an old wife, and
old dog, and ready money.
—BENJAMIN FRANKLIN

*Y*ou can always tell a real friend: When you've
made a fool of yourself he doesn't feel you've
done a permanent job.
—LAURENCE J. PETER

*F*riendship with the wise gets better with time, as a good book gets better with age.
———Thiruvalluvar

A hedge between keeps friendship green.
———English proverb

A friend that ain't in need is a friend indeed.
———Kin Hubbard

I don't like to commit myself about heaven and hell—you see, I have friends in both places.
———Mark Twain

Good friends are good for your health.
—IRWIN SARASON

Love thy neighbor as thyself, but choose your
neighborhood.
—LOUISE BEAL

My best friend is the man who in wishing me
well wishes it for my sake.
—ARISTOTLE

No friend's a friend till he shall prove a friend.
—BEAUMONT AND FLETCHER

The truth that is suppressed by friends is the
readiest weapon of the enemy.
——ROBERT LOUIS STEVENSON

The condition which high friendship demands
is ability to do without it.
——RALPH WALDO EMERSON

Friendship is honey—but don't eat it all.
——MOROCCAN PROVERB

One loyal friend is worth ten thousand relatives.
——EURIPIDES

*I*f we were all given by magic the power to read
each other's thoughts, I suppose the first effect
would be to dissolve all friendships.
—BERTRAND RUSSELL

*A*gainst a foe I can myself defend,—
But Heaven protect me from a blundering friend!
—D'ARCY W. THOMPSON

*T*he essence of true friendship is to make
allowance for another's little lapses.
—DAVID STOREY

A true friend will see you through when others
see that you are through.
———Laurence J. Peter

*C*onvey thy love to thy friend as an arrow to the
mark, to stick there, not as a ball against the
wall, to rebound back to thee.
———Francis Quarles

*T*rue friendship comes when silence between two
people is comfortable.
———David Tyson Gentry

My wife once said that she likes me to be at home, in my own study. She doesn't want to talk to me, or to see me, but she likes to think I'm there. That's exactly how I feel about the small number of my oldest friends.

—SIR WALTER RALEIGH

A friend is a speaking acquaintance who also listens.

—ARTHUR H. GLASGOW

Friendship is a plant we must often water.

—GERMAN PROVERB

In friendship we find nothing false or insincere;
everything is straightforward, and springs
from the heart.

—CICERO

Rather the bite of a friend than the kiss of an
enemy.

—SHALOM ALEICHEM

Better a nettle in the side of your friend than
his echo.

—RALPH WALDO EMERSON

No man is the whole of himself. His friends are
the rest of him.
—PROVERB

I am treating you as my friend, asking you to
share my present minuses in the hope that I
can ask you to share my future pluses.
—KATHERINE MANSFIELD

A friend at one's back is a safe bridge.
—DUTCH SAYING

*E*very man should have a fair-sized cemetery in
which to bury the faults of his friends.

—HENRY BROOKS ADAMS

*F*riendship is not a fruit for enjoyment only, but
also an opportunity for service.

—GREEK PROVERB

*T*he more we love our friends, the less we flatter
them; it is by excusing nothing that pure love
shows itself.

—JEAN-BAPTISTE MOLIÈRE

One who looks for a friend without faults will
have none.
—HASIDIC SAYING

If the first law of friendship is that it has to be
cultivated, the second law is to be indulgent
when the first law has been neglected.
—VOLTAIRE

Friendship will not stand the strain of very much
good advice for very long.
—ROBERT LYND

*Y*ou cannot be friends upon any other terms than
upon the terms of equality.
—WOODROW WILSON

*T*rue happiness
Consists not in the multitude of friends,
But in the worth and choice.
—BEN JONSON

A good friend—like a tube of toothpaste—
comes through in a tight squeeze.
—ANONYMOUS

We make our friends; we make our enemies; but God makes our next-door neighbour.

—G. K. CHESTERTON

Friendship is not possible between two women, one of whom is very well dressed.

—LAURIE COLWIN

Friends do not live in harmony merely, as some say, but in melody.

—HENRY DAVID THOREAU

My best friend is the one who brings out the best in me.

— HENRY FORD

She's my best friend. I hate her.

— RICHMAL CROMPTON

We have fewer friends than we imagine, but more than we know.

— HUGO VON HOFMANNSTHAL

*O*f what help is anyone who can only be
approached with the right words?
—ELIZABETH BIBESCO

*S*ometimes, with luck, we find the kind of true
friend, male or female, that appears only two
or three times in a lucky lifetime, one that will
winter us and summer us, grieve, rejoice, and
travel with us.
—BARBARA HOLLAND

*T*he best time to make friends is before you need
them.
—ETHEL BARRYMORE

Constant use had not worn ragged the fabric of
their friendship.
—DOROTHY PARKER

True friendship is like sound health; the value of it
is seldom known until it be lost.
—CHARLES CALEB COLTON

The friendships which last are those wherein each
friend respects the other's dignity to the point
of not really wanting anything from him.
—CYRIL CONNOLLY

*I*n time of prosperity friends will be plenty;
in time of adversity not one in twenty.
———ENGLISH PROVERB

*W*hen someone tells you the truth, lets you think
for yourself, experience your own emotions, he
is treating you as a true equal. As a friend.
———WHITNEY OTTO

I set out to find a friend but couldn't find one;
I set out to be a friend, and friends were
everywhere.
———ANONYMOUS

I desire so to conduct the affairs of this adminis-
tration that if at the end, when I come to lay
down the reins of power, I have lost every
other friend on earth, I shall at least have one
friend left, and that friend shall be down inside
of me.

—ABRAHAM LINCOLN

I had only one friend, my dog. My wife was mad
at me, and I told her a man ought to have at
least two friends. She agreed—and bought me
another dog.

—PEPPER RODGERS

*T*reat your friends as you do your pictures, and
place them in their best light.
——JENNIE JEROME CHURCHILL

*D*on't put your friend in your pocket.
——IRISH PROVERB

A friend of man was he, and thus, he was a
friend of God.
——WILSON MACDONALD

*I*n my friend, I find a second self.
——ISABEL NORTON

*H*owever rare true love may be, it is less so than true friendship.
—LA ROCHEFOUCAULD

*O*ne friend in a lifetime is much; two are many; three are hardly possible.
—HENRY ADAMS

A new friend is like new wine; when it has aged you will drink it with pleasure.
—APOCRYPHA, ECCLESIASTICUS

*I*f we would build on a sure foundation in friendship, we must love friends for their sake rather than for our own.

—CHARLOTTE BRONTË

I keep my friends as misers do their treasure, because, of all the things granted us by wisdom, none is greater or better than friendship.

—PIETRO ARETINO

*T*he firmest friendships have been formed in mutual adversity, as iron is most strongly united by the fiercest flame.

—CHARLES CALEB COLTON

*F*riends show their love
in times of trouble, not in happiness.
—EURIPIDES

*N*obody who is afraid of laughing, and heartily
too, at his friend, can be said to have a true and
thorough love for him.
—JULIUS CHARLES HARE AND
AUGUSTUS WILLIAM HARE

*O*ne cannot help using his early friends as the
seaman uses the log, to mark his progress.
—OLIVER WENDELL HOLMES SR.

A sympathetic friend can be quite as dear as a brother.

—HOMER

*T*hat friendship may be at once fond and lasting, there must not only be equal virtue on each part, but virtue of the same kind; not only the same end must be proposed, but the same means must be approved by both.

—SAMUEL JOHNSON

*F*ate makes our relatives, choice makes our friends.

—JACQUES DELILLE

A friend may well be reckoned the masterpiece of nature.

—RALPH WALDO EMERSON

*H*old a true friend with both your hands.

—NIGERIAN PROVERB

*L*ife is partly what we make it, and partly what it is made by the friends whom we choose.

—TEHYI HSIEH

*I*f I don't have friends, then I ain't got nothin'.

—BILLIE HOLIDAY

*T*rue friendship is never serene.

———MARIE DE RABUTIN-CHANTAL

*I*t is characteristic of spontaneous friendships to
take on first, without enquiry and almost at
first sight, the unseen doings and unspoken
sentiments of our friends; the parts known give
us evidence enough that the unknown parts
cannot be much amiss.

———GEORGE SANTAYANA

*T*he perfect friendship is that between good men,
alike in their virtue.

———ARISTOTLE

*F*riendship always benefits; love sometimes injures.

— SENECA

*Y*ou can keep your friends by not giving them away.

— MARY PETTIBONE POOLE

*T*here was a definite process by which one made people into friends, and it involved talking to them and listening to them for hours at a time.

— REBECCA WEST

A woman's friendship borders more closely on love than man's. Men affect each other in the reflection of noble or friendly acts; whilst women ask fewer proofs and more signs and expressions of attachment.

—SAMUEL TAYLOR COLERIDGE

*I*t is the friends that you can call at 4 A.M. that matter.

—MARLENE DIETRICH

*W*hy do people lament their follies for which their friends adore them?

—GERARD HOPKINS

"Stay" is a charming word in a friend's
vocabulary.
—LOUISA MAY ALCOTT

Animals are such agreeable friends, they ask
no questions, they pass no criticisms.
—GEORGE ELIOT

To attract good fortune, spend a new penny on an
old friend, share an old pleasure with a new
friend, and lift up the heart of a true friend by
writing his name on the wings of a dragon.
—CHINESE PROVERB

*I*f a man does not make new acquaintance as he
advances through life, he will soon find himself
left alone. A man, sir, should keep his friendship in constant repair.

—SAMUEL JOHNSON

*T*hough friendship is not quick to burn,
It is explosive stuff.

—MAY SARTON

A friend is in prosperitie a pleasure, a solace in
aduersitie, in grief a comfort, in joy a merry
companion, at al times an other I.

—JOHN LYLY

*F*riendship is like two clocks keeping time.
—ANONYMOUS

*T*wo friendships in two breasts requires
The same aversions and desires.
—JONATHAN SWIFT

A faithful friend is the medicine of life.
—APOCRYPHA,
ECCLESIASTICUS

*H*ave no friends not equal to yourself.
—CONFUCIUS

*H*ave patience with a friend rather than lose him
forever.
—ARAB PROVERB

A faithful friend is a strong protection;
A man who has found one has found a treasure.
A faithful friend is beyond price,
And his value cannot be weighed.
—BEN SIRA

*W*e cherish our friends not for their ability to
amuse us, but for ours to amuse them.
—EVELYN WAUGH

To find a friend one must close one eye—to keep
   him, two.
                    —NORMAN DOUGLAS

The best mirror is an old friend.
                    —GEORGE HERBERT

I am not of that feather to shake off
My friend when he most need me.
                    —WILLIAM SHAKESPEARE

There is nothing final between friends.
—William Jennings Bryan

You meet your friend, your face brightens—you have struck gold.
—Kassia

For what do my friends stand? Not for the clever things they say: I do not remember them half an hour after they are spoken. It is the unspoken, the unconscious, which is their reality to me.
—Mark Rutherford

*T*rue friends visit us in prosperity only when invited, but in adversity they come without invitation.

—THEOPHRASTUS

A friend is a gift you give yourself.

—ROBERT LOUIS STEVENSON

A stone from the hand of a friend is an apple.

—MOROCCAN PROVERB

Odd how much it hurts when a friend moves
away—and leaves behind only silence.
—Pam Brown

Oh, the comfort, the inexpressible comfort of
feeling safe with a person, having neither to
weigh thoughts nor measure words, but
pouring them all right out, just as they are,
chaff and grain together; certain that a faithful
hand will take and sift them, keep what is
worth keeping, and then with the breath of
kindness throw the rest away.
—Dinah Maria Mulock Craik

*D*evelop the art of friendliness. One can experience a variety of emotions staying home and reading or watching television; one will be alive but hardly living. Most of the meaningful aspects of life are closely associated with people. Even the dictionary definition of life involves people.
—WILLIAM L. ABBOTT

*T*he holy passion of friendship is so sweet and steady and loyal and enduring in nature that it will last through a whole lifetime, if not asked to lend money.
—MARK TWAIN

*W*herever you are it is your own friends who
make your world.

—WILLIAM JAMES

*T*rouble is a sieve through which we sift our
acquaintances. Those too big to pass through
are our friends.

—ARLENE FRANCIS

A home-made friend wears longer than one you
buy in the market.

—AUSTIN O'MALLEY

The glory of Friendship is not the outstretched hand, nor the kindly smile, nor the joy of companionship; it is the spiritual inspiration that comes to one when he discovers that someone else believes in him and is willing to trust him with his friendship.

—RALPH WALDO EMERSON

A home-made friend wears longer than one you buy in the market.

—AUSTIN O'MALLEY

To have a good friend is one of the highest delights of life; to be a good friend is one of the noblest and most difficult undertakings.

—ANONYMOUS

The two most important things in life are good friends and a strong bullpen.

—BOB LEMON

Friendship is the only cement that will ever hold the world together.

—WOODROW WILSON

The worst solitude is to be destitute of sincere friendship.

—FRANCIS BACON

My friends have made the story of my life. In a thousand ways they have turned my limitations into beautiful privileges.

—HELEN KELLER

Don't ask of your friends what you can do yourself.

—QUINTUS ENNIUS

We cannot tell the precise moment when friendship is formed. As in filling a vessel drop by
drop, there is at last a drop which makes it
run over. So in a series of kindnesses there is,
at last, one which makes the heart run over.
——JAMES BOSWELL

Friends are like a pleasant park where you may
wish to go; while you may enjoy the flowers,
you may not eat them.
——EDGAR HOWE

Friendship is like money, easier made than kept.
——SAMUEL BUTLER

*K*eep the other person's well-being in mind
when you feel an attack of soul-purging truth
coming on.
———BETTY WHITE

I love you not only for what you have made of
yourself, but for what you are making of me.
———ROY CROFT

*W*hen you are young and without success,
you have only a few friends. Then, later on,
when you are rich and famous, you still have
a few . . . if you are lucky.
———PABLO PICASSO

If it's very painful for you to criticize your
friends—you're safe in doing it. But if you take
the slightest pleasure in it, that's the time to
hold your tongue.
—ALICE DUER MILLER

He alone has lost the art to live who cannot win
new friends.
—S. WEIR MITCHELL

Better fare hard with good men than feast
with bad.
—THOMAS FULLER, M.D.

That friendship will not continue to the end which
is begun for an end.
—Francis Quarles

The most beautiful discovery true friends can
make is that they can grow separately without
growing apart.
—Elizabeth Foley

Love

If you'd be loved, be worthy to be loved.
—Ovid

Love consists in this, that two solitudes protect
and border and salute each other.
—Rainer Maria Rilke

The affirmative of affirmatives is love.
—Ralph Waldo Emerson

The pounding of your heart in romance and the
    pounding of your heart in danger are perhaps
    the same thing.
                    —MICHAEL LEVINE

'Tis better to have loved and lost
Than never to have loved at all.
                    —ALFRED, LORD TENNYSON

The absolute value of love makes life worth while,
    and so makes Man's strange and difficult
    situation acceptable. Love cannot save life
    from death; but it can fulfill life's purpose.
                    —ARNOLD J. TOYNBEE

*W*ho, being loved, is poor?
— OSCAR WILDE

*L*et the dead have the immortality of fame, but the living the immortality of love.
— RABINDRANATH TAGORE

*L*ove is the subtlest force in the world.
— MAHATMA GANDHI

*L*ove and dignity cannot share the same abode.
— OVID

*F*ew people know what they mean when they say, "I love you." . . . Well, what does the word *love* mean? It means total interest. I think the reason very few people really fall in love with anyone is they're not willing to pay the price. The price is you have to adjust yourself to them.

—KATHARINE HEPBURN

*L*ove is such a funny thing;
    It's very like a lizard;
It twines itself round the heart
    And penetrates your gizzard.

—ANONYMOUS

*A*s a romance ends, women don't hurt more
than men, just differently.
—MICHAEL LEVINE

*I*t is a curious thought, but it is only when you see
people looking ridiculous, that you realize just
how much you love them.
—AGATHA CHRISTIE

*B*y accident of fortune a man may rule the world
for a time, but by virtue of love he may rule the
world forever.
—LAO-TZU

*W*e can only learn to love by loving.
———IRIS MURDOCH

*I*ntellect, in its effort to explain Love, got stuck in the mud like an ass. Love alone could explain love and loving.
———RUMI

*W*e can perhaps learn to prepare for love. We can welcome its coming, we can learn to treasure and cherish it when it comes, but we cannot make it happen. We are elected into love.
———IRENE CLAREMONT DE CASTILLEJO

*F*or one human being to love another: that is
perhaps the most difficult of all our tasks, the
ultimate, the last test and proof, the work for
which all other work is but preparation.
—RAINER MARIA RILKE

*L*ove is the only gold.
—ALFRED, LORD TENNYSON

*T*here is no remedy for love but to love more.
—HENRY DAVID THOREAU

Love is the only force capable of transforming an enemy into a friend.
—MARTIN LUTHER KING JR.

One of the oldest human needs is having someone to wonder where you are when you don't come home at night.
—MARGARET MEAD

Love doesn't have to feel dizzying.
—MICHAEL LEVINE

*W*hen a chap is in love, he will go out in all kinds of weather to keep an appointment with his beloved. Love can be demanding, in fact more demanding than law. It has its own imperatives—think of a mother sitting by the bedside of a sick child through the night, impelled only by love. Nothing is too much trouble for love.

———DESMOND TUTU

*L*ove for the joy of loving, and not for the offerings of someone else's heart.

———MARLENE DIETRICH

*L*ove has nothing to do with what you are
    expecting to get—only what you are expecting
    to give—which is everything. What you will
    receive in return varies. But it really has no
    connection with what you give. You give
    because you love and cannot help giving. If you
    are very lucky, you may be loved back. That is
    delicious, but it does not necessarily happen.
              —KATHARINE HEPBURN

*W*e find love only when we give love to others.
              —DOUGLAS M. LAWSON

*L*ove is something like the clouds that were in the sky before the sun came out. You cannot touch the clouds, you know; but you feel the rain and know how glad the flowers and the thirsty earth are to have it after a hot day. You cannot touch love either; but you feel the sweetness that it pours into everything.

—ANNIE SULLIVAN

*L*ove knows hidden paths.

—GERMAN PROVERB

*L*ove is never abstract. It does not adhere to the universe of the planet or the nation or the institution or the profession, but to the singular sparrows of the street, the lilies of the field, "the least of these my brethren." Love is not, by its own desire, heroic. It is heroic only when compelled to be. It exists by its willingness to be anonymous, humble, and unrewarded.

—WENDELL BERRY

*M*aking the decision to have a child—it's momentous. It is to decide forever to have your heart go walking around outside your body.

—ELIZABETH STONE

*L*ife is an attitude. Have a good one.
—ERIC L. LUNGAARD

A life without love, without the presence of the beloved, is nothing but a mere magic-lantern show. We draw out slide after slide, swiftly tiring of each, and pushing it back to make haste for the next.
—JOHANN WOLFGANG VON GOETHE

*L*ove is that condition in which the happiness of another person is essential to your own.
—ROBERT A. HEINLEIN

*P*eople need loving the most when they deserve
 it the least.
—MARY CROWLEY

*L*ove and time are the only two things in this
 world that cannot be bought, only spent.
—GARY JENNINGS

*L*ove possesses seven hundred wings, and each
 one extends from the highest heaven to the
 lowest earth.
—RUMI

*S*ympathy constitutes friendship; but in love there is a sort of antipathy, or opposing passion. Each strives to be the other, and both together make up one whole.

—SAMUEL TAYLOR COLERIDGE

*T*he richest love is that which submits to the arbitration of time.

—LAWRENCE DURRELL

*L*ove is Nature's second sun.

—GEORGE CHAPMAN

*L*ove talked about can be easily turned aside,
but love demonstrated is irresistible.
—W. STANLEY MOONEYHAM

*L*ove is a power, like money, or steam, or
electricity. It is valueless unless you can give
something else by means of it.
—ANNE MORROW LINDBERGH

*A*mong those whom I like or admire, I can find
no common denominator, but among those
whom I love, I can: all of them make me laugh.
—W. H. AUDEN

*W*hoso loves
Believes the impossible.
———Elizabeth Barrett
Browning

*T*rue love comes quietly, without banners or
flashing lights. If you hear bells, get your
ears checked.
———Erich Segal

*T*he love we give away is the only love we keep.
———Elbert Hubbard

*L*ove is love's reward.
——JOHN DRYDEN

I define love thus: The will to extend one's self
for the purpose of nurturing one's own or
another's spiritual growth.
——M. SCOTT PECK

*E*ffort matters in everything, love included.
Learning to love is purposeful work.
——MICHAEL LEVINE

*T*he Eskimos had fifty-two names for snow
   because snow was important to them: there
   ought to be as many for love.
                   —MARGARET ATWOOD

*T*o love and be loved is to feel the sun from
   both sides.
                   —DAVID VISCOTT

*L*ove is all we have, the only way
that each can help the other.
                   —EURIPIDES

*L*ove is the true price of love.
— GEORGE HERBERT

*W*hoever loves true life, will love true love.
— ELIZABETH BARRETT
BROWNING

*L*ove is an energy which exists of itself. It is its
own value.
— THORNTON WILDER

*W*e don't love qualities, we love persons; sometimes by reason of their defects as well as of their qualities.
———JACQUES MARITAIN

*L*ove dies only when growth stops.
———PEARL S. BUCK

*T*he supreme happiness of life is the conviction that we are loved.
———VICTOR HUGO

As selfishness and complaint pervert and cloud the mind, so love with its joy clears and sharpens the vision.
—HELEN KELLER

It is love, not reason, that is stronger than death.
—THOMAS MANN

'Tis never for their wisdom that one loves the wisest, or for their wit that one loves the wittiest; 'tis for benevolence and virtue and honest fondness one loves people.
—HESTER LYNCH PIOZZI

*L*ove is not dumb. The heart speaks many ways.
———RACINE

*T*he loving are the daring.
———BAYARD TAYLOR

*O*ne cannot be strong without love. For love is
not an irrelevant emotion; it is the blood of life,
the power of reunion of the separated.
———PAUL TILLICH

*L*ove doesn't just sit there, like a stone, it has
   to be made, like bread; remade all the time,
   made new.

—URSULA K. LE GUIN

*L*ove withers under constraint: its very essence is
   liberty: it is compatible neither with obedience,
   jealousy, nor fear: it is there most pure, perfect,
   and unlimited where its votaries live in confidence, equality and unreserve.

—PERCY BYSSHE SHELLEY

*L*ove is not self-sacrifice, but the most profound
  assertion of your own needs and values. It is for
  your *own* happiness that you need the person
  you love, and that is the greatest compliment,
  the greatest tribute you can pay to that person.
  —AYN RAND

I may have all knowledge and understand all
  secrets; I may have all the faith needed
To move mountains—but if I have no love,
  I am nothing.
  —I CORINTHIANS 13:2

*W*hilst in this land
Of fruitless pursuits,
you are always unbalanced, always
either all back or all front;
but once the seeking soul has progressed
just a few paces beyond this state,
love seizes the reins.

—AL-HAKIM

*T*hose who would know much, and love little,
will ever remain at but the beginning of a
godly life.

—MECHTILD OF MAGDEBURG

If thou wish to reach the perfection of love,
   it befits thee to set thy life in order.
                    —CATHERINE OF SIENA

To be loved, love.
                    —DECIMUS MAGNUS AUSONIUS

Love looks through a telescope; envy, through
   a microscope.
                    —JOSH BILLINGS

All, everything that I understand, I understand only because I love.
——LEO TOLSTOY

Love spends his all, and still hath store.
——PHILIP JAMES BAILEY

Of all earthly music, that which reaches farthest into heaven is the beating of a truly loving heart.
——HENRY WARD BEECHER

*L*ook round our world; behold the chain of love
Combining all below and all above.
—ALEXANDER POPE

*T*he best way to know God is to love many things.
—VINCENT VAN GOGH

*L*ove, like the opening of the heavens to the
saints, shows for a moment, even to the dullest
man, the possibilities of the human race.
—SIR ARTHUR HELPS

God hears no sweeter music than the cracked chimes of the courageous human spirit ringing in imperfect acknowledgement of His perfect love.

—JOSHUA LOTH LIEBMAN

Faith, like light, should always be simple and unbending; while love, like warmth, should beam forth on every side, and bend to every necessity of our brethren.

—MARTIN LUTHER

A pennyweight of love is worth a pound of law.

—SCOTTISH PROVERB

*L*ove is free.

— GEOFFREY CHAUCER

*F*or finally, we are as we love. It is love that
measures our stature.

— WILLIAM SLOANE COFFIN

THE TEXT OF THIS BOOK IS SET IN GRANJON
BY MSPACE, KATONAH, NEW YORK.

BOOK DESIGN BY MAURA FADDEN ROSENTHAL